WEATHER and CLIMATE

How Weather Works

Robin Birch

MACMILLAN
LIBRARY

First published in 2009 by
MACMILLAN EDUCATION AUSTRALIA PTY LTD
15–19 Claremont Street, South Yarra 3141

Visit our website at www.macmillan.com.au or go directly to www.macmillanlibrary.com.au
Associated companies and representatives throughout the world.

Copyright © Robin Birch 2009

All rights reserved.
Except under the conditions described in the *Copyright Act 1968* of Australia
and subsequent amendments, no part of this publication may be reproduced,
stored in a retrieval system, or transmitted in any form or by any means,
electronic, mechanical, photocopying, recording or otherwise, without the
prior written permission of the copyright owner.

Educational institutions copying any part of this book for educational purposes
under the Act must be covered by a Copyright Agency Limited (CAL) licence
for educational institutions and must have given a remuneration notice to CAL.
Licence restrictions must be adhered to. Any copies must be photocopies only,
and they must not be hired out or sold. For details of the CAL licence contact:
Copyright Agency Limited, Level 15, 233 Castlereagh Street, Sydney, NSW 2000.
Telephone: (02) 9394 7600. Facsimile: (02) 9394 7601. Email: info@copyright.com.au

National Library of Australia Cataloguing-in-Publication data

Birch, Robin.
 How weather works / Robin Birch.

 9781420265989 (hbk.)
 Weather and climate.
 Includes index.
 For primary school age.
 Weather - Juvenile literature
  Meteorology - Juvenile literature
551.8

Edited by Kylie Cockle
Text and cover design by Marta White
Page layout by Marta White
Photo research by Legend Images
Illustrations by Gaston Vanzet

Printed in China

Acknowledgements
The author and the publisher are grateful to the following for permission to reproduce copyright material:
Front cover photograph: Cumulonimbus thunderclouds © Condor 36/Shutterstock
Photos courtesy of:
Dreamstime.com, **5**; © Maco0708/Dreamstime.com, **22** (left); © Photosbyash/Dreamstime.com, **27** (bottom); © Zvonkomir/Dreamstime.com, **4**; Christopher Pillitz/Getty Images, **27** (top); Jochen Schlenker/Getty Images, **15**; © Andreas Karelias/iStockphoto, **19** (left); © Tor Lindqvist/iStockphoto, **21** (top); © Tim Messick/iStockphoto, **28**; © Drazen Vukelic/iStockphoto, **21** (bottom); NASA, **25**; NASA/JSC, **7**; SeaWiFS Project, NASA/Goddard Space Flight Center, and ORBIMAGE, **29**; NOAA, photo by Captain Albert E. Theberge Jr., NOAA Corps (ret.), **14** (top); NOAA/AOML/Hurricane Research Division, **14** (bottom); Photolibrary/Gene Moore, **18**; Photolibrary/Elisabeth Sauer, **19** (top right); © Alexey Avdeev/Shutterstock, **22** (right); © Can Balcioglu/Shutterstock, **12** (top right); © Peter Baxter/Shutterstock, **12** (top left), **20**; © Condor 36/Shutterstock, **16**; © Dainis Derics/Shutterstock, **19** (bottom right); © bruno ismael da silva alves/Shutterstock, **12** (bottom); © Holger Mette/Shutterstock, **8**; © vhpfoto/Shutterstock, **30**.

While every care has been taken to trace and acknowledge copyright, the publisher tenders their apologies for any accidental infringement where copyright has proved untraceable. Where the attempt has been unsuccessful, the publisher welcomes information that would redress the situation.

Contents

Glossary Words

When a word is printed in **bold**, you can look up its meaning in the Glossary on page 31.

Weather and climate

What is the weather like today? Is it hot, cold, wet, dry, windy or still? Is it frosty or snowy? Is there a storm on the way? We are all interested in the weather, because it makes a difference to how we feel, what we wear and what we can do.

The weather takes place in the air, and we notice it because air is all around us.

Climate

The word 'climate' describes the usual weather of a particular place. If a place usually has cold weather, then we say that place has a cold climate. If a place usually has hot weather, we say it has a hot climate.

Weather Report

Sailors and fishermen need to know whether it is safe to be on the water. Strong winds can blow the water into big waves that can tip boats over.

Sailing can be fun in the right kind of weather.

How weather works

Earth has a layer of air around it. This layer of air is called the 'atmosphere'. All of Earth's weather takes place in the atmosphere. Weather is caused by:

- Earth **orbiting** the Sun
- Earth spinning
- the Sun heating Earth's atmosphere, lands and oceans
- the shape of the lands and oceans on Earth.

What do we notice about the weather?

We can watch the weather to learn more about how it works.

If we notice ...	we are noticing ...
how hot or cold the air is	temperature
how moist or dry the air is	humidity
that the air is moving	wind
that rain, hail or snow is falling	precipitation

Meteorology

The study of weather is called 'meteorology'. Scientists who study the weather and how it works are known as 'meteorologists'.

A meteorologist checks data in order to prepare a weather forecast.

The atmosphere

Earth is surrounded by a layer of air known as the 'atmosphere'. The air in the atmosphere is thickest at the ground level and gets thinner and thinner until it joins with outer space.

Layers in the atmosphere

The atmosphere has four layers in it. From the surface of Earth, these layers are:

- troposphere
- stratosphere
- mesosphere
- thermosphere.

Troposphere

The troposphere makes up half of Earth's atmosphere, because the air is thicker here than in the other layers. The troposphere is the layer in which nearly all of Earth's weather occurs. Stormy conditions take place in the troposphere. This layer contains a lot of dust and **water vapour**. Temperatures range from 15 degrees Celsius to minus 55 degrees Celsius.

Weather Report

The average temperature at the bottom of the troposphere is 15 degrees **Celsius**. The troposphere gets colder with increasing height.

500 kilometres

thermosphere

80 kilometres

mesosphere

50 kilometres

stratosphere

8-15 kilometres

troposphere

Layers of the atmosphere

Stratosphere

The stratosphere is above the troposphere. This layer has dry air and it becomes warmer further out from Earth. Jet aircraft often fly though this layer, as the air is stable. The **ozone** in the stratosphere soaks up dangerous **rays** of **ultraviolet (UV) light** from the Sun.

Mesosphere

In the mesosphere, the air becomes colder further away from Earth. Temperatures can drop to minus 100 degrees Celsius. **Meteors** usually burn up in the mesosphere entering Earth's atmosphere. Meteors are also known as 'shooting stars'.

Thermosphere

The thermosphere is the outer layer of the atmosphere and the air is very thin here. Temperatures can reach 2000 degrees Celsius. This is where we find meteor trails, and it is where spacecraft orbit Earth.

A photo of Earth taken from a spacecraft. The blue band around the Earth is the atmosphere.

The Sun

The Sun is a star and it is the centre of our **solar system**. It is the nearest star to Earth and is a glowing ball of **gases** that heats and lights up Earth. The Sun causes most of Earth's weather because it heats its lands, water and atmosphere.

The Sun's rays

The Sun gives off different types of rays. Some of them are dangerous. Earth's atmosphere blocks most of the dangerous rays, so they cannot reach the ground and affect humans, plants and animals.

Rays from the Sun and what they do

Type of rays	What the rays do
infra-red	Infra-red rays heat up the atmosphere and ground.
light	Light rays light up the atmosphere and ground.
ultraviolet	Ultraviolet rays can cause sunburn. Most ultraviolet rays cannot pass through the atmosphere.
gamma	Gamma rays cannot pass through the atmosphere.
X-ray	X-rays cannot pass through the atmosphere.
radio waves	Radio wave rays pass through the atmosphere, and can reach the ground.

Weather Report

The Australian Bureau of Meteorology issues a UV Index forecast every day to help people to avoid exposure to UV radiation. If the UV level is 3 or above, your skin can be damaged.

This area is on Earth's equator, so it gets a lot of sunlight. It has warm weather all year.

Seasons

Earth orbits the Sun, taking a year to complete a full orbit. Earth is tilted on its **axis**. This gives Earth its seasons during the year.

Summer and winter

When Earth's **North Pole** is tilted towards the Sun, the Northern **Hemisphere** becomes warmer than the Southern Hemisphere. This causes summer in the Northern Hemisphere and winter in the Southern Hemisphere.

When Earth's **South Pole** is tilted towards the Sun, the Southern Hemisphere becomes warmer than the Northern Hemisphere. This causes summer in the Southern Hemisphere and winter in the Northern Hemisphere.

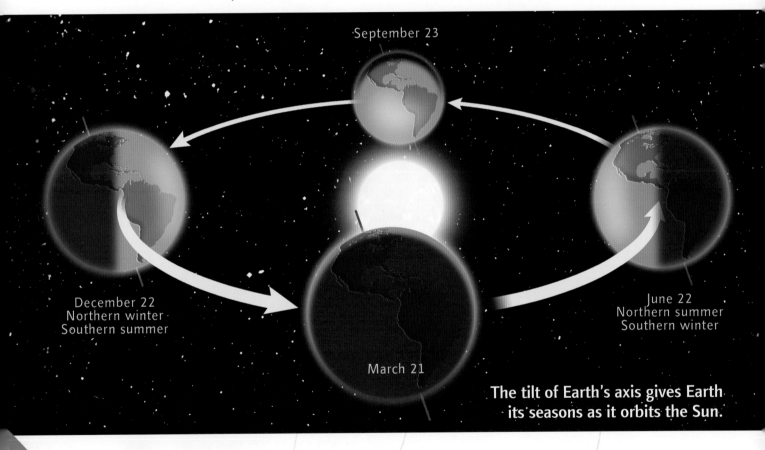

September 23

December 22
Northern winter
Southern summer

March 21

June 22
Northern summer
Southern winter

The tilt of Earth's axis gives Earth its seasons as it orbits the Sun.

The equator

The equator is an imaginary line around the middle of Earth's surface. It is an equal distance from the North Pole and the South Pole. In areas on or near Earth's equator, the Sun is always overhead or nearly overhead. These places have warm weather all year. Many of them have wet and dry seasons.

The Sun and the atmosphere

When the Sun shines on Earth, the atmosphere:

- reflects some of the Sun's heat and light **radiation**
- soaks up some of the Sun's heat and light radiation
- lets some of the Sun's heat and light radiation through to the ground.

The ozone layer

The ozone layer is a layer of ozone gas in the lower half of the stratosphere. This ozone layer absorbs dangerous ultraviolet rays from the Sun. It is an extremely important layer as it protects all living things from most of these dangerous rays.

Ultraviolet light

The ozone layer does not filter out all the invisible ultraviolet light from the Sun. Some rays still get through the atmosphere. These rays can damage people's eyes and can also cause skin cancer. This is the main reason why we are encouraged to wear a hat and sunblock, and to stay out of the Sun between 10 a.m. and 3 p.m. in summertime.

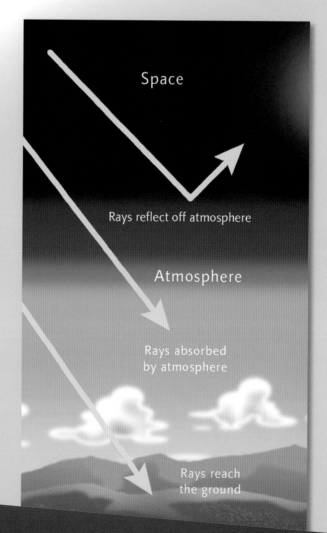

Space

Rays reflect off atmosphere

Atmosphere

Rays absorbed by atmosphere

Rays reach the ground

The atmosphere does not let all of the Sun's radiation reach the ground.

The greenhouse effect

The atmosphere acts like a blanket around Earth. Much of the heat and light from the Sun reaches the ground, and is reflected back up to space. However, the atmosphere stops some of this heat from escaping. This process is called the 'greenhouse effect'.

Today, there is more **carbon dioxide** in the atmosphere than there used to be. More carbon dioxide means the atmosphere soaks up more warmth and causes land and water temperatures to increase. This effect is called the 'enhanced greenhouse effect'.

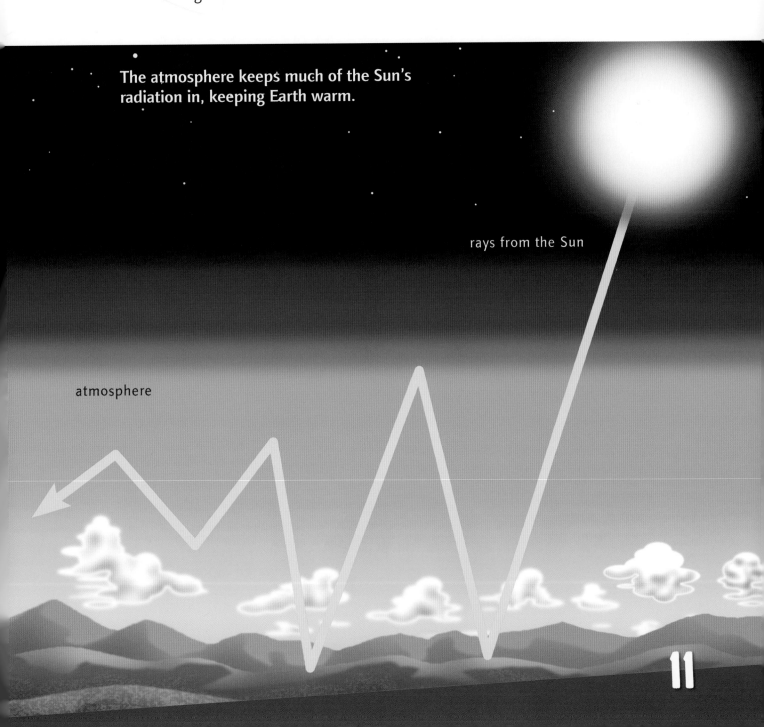

The atmosphere keeps much of the Sun's radiation in, keeping Earth warm.

rays from the Sun

atmosphere

Water

There is water both on Earth's surface and in the atmosphere. Much of our weather consists of water moving about.

Solid, liquid and gas

Water can exist in three different forms. These are solid, liquid and gas.

Facts about water

- We cannot see water vapour because it is made of particles that are very small and far apart, like other gases. When liquid water becomes water vapour, the vapour mixes with the air, which is also a gas.

- When liquid water is heated and becomes water vapour, we say it evaporates.

- When water vapour is cooled and becomes a liquid, we say it condenses.

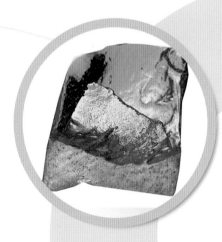

If liquid water freezes it becomes solid water, or ice.

Water that comes out of a tap is in liquid form.

If liquid water is heated, it turns into a gas, or water vapour.

Water in the atmosphere

Air contains water vapour. This water vapour comes from water that has evaporated from seas, lakes, rivers and streams.

The amount of water vapour in the air is called 'humidity'. Although we cannot see water vapour, we can measure the air's humidity. When air has a high humidity we feel sticky. When humidity is low, we feel more comfortable, even if it is hot.

Weather Report

We perspire when it is hot because our perspiration cools us down as it evaporates. When humidity is high our perspiration cannot evaporate as well, so we feel sticky.

Dew and frost

At night, the ground and the air above it cools down. In cold weather, the air cools down so much that water vapour in the air condenses back into water drops. This makes small drops of water settle on the ground and on plants and other objects. These water drops are called 'dew'. If it is very cold, the small drops of water freeze and make frost.

All water on Earth circulates in a never-ending process called 'the water cycle'.

Sun

Some of the water vapour condenses to make clouds.

wind

snow

Water falls from the clouds as rain and runs back to the sea.

Heat from the sun evaporates water from the seas, lakes, rivers and streams.

rain

Snow melts and runs back to the sea

Clouds

Clouds are made of tiny water drops or ice **crystals** that are so lightweight that they float in the air. They form when warm air rises and then cools down, so that the water vapour in this air condenses or freezes.

Air may rise because it:

- is warmed by the land or sea
- is pushed up by colder air that is moving in underneath it
- flows over the top of colder air
- is pushed up the side of a mountain by wind.

Clouds usually only form in air that has tiny particles in it, such as dust, salt or smoke. The water vapour can stick to these particles.

These cirrus clouds are made of ice crystals.

These cumulus clouds are made of tiny water drops.

Fog and mist

Fog is low cloud that reaches down to the ground or water. It forms in a different way from clouds that are high in the sky. Most fog is made from tiny water drops, but in extremely cold places it can be made from ice crystals – this is called 'ice fog'.

Fog usually forms when moist air is cooled by the ground below it. Cold air does not rise, so it is trapped close to the ground until the Sun warms it.

Mist is fog made from very tiny water drops. It is not as thick as fog, and we can see through it more easily.

Weather Report

Sea fog can form in fairly dry air, because the water drops form around salt particles. This kind of fog blows over San Francisco.

This valley fog formed because the ground was cold overnight in the valley.

Types of clouds

All clouds are found in the troposphere, which is the lowest layer of the atmosphere. The troposphere is, overall, warmest at the bottom and it becomes very cold at the top. Clouds are named according to their height, shape and what they contain.

Cloud names

Names have been given to the different types of clouds. These names come from Latin and they describe five main types of cloud.

Words, or parts of words, used in cloud names

Word or part of word	Describes clouds that ...
cirrus (cirro)	are made of ice crystals
cumulus (cumulo)	are heaped
nimbus (nimbo)	bring rain
stratus (strato)	make flat layers
alto	are higher up

Other cloud types can be described by joining these words in different combinations. For example, cumulonimbus is a type of rain cloud that is heaped and brings rain.

Cumulus clouds

On a warm, sunny day we often see clouds that look like cotton balls. They are flat across the bottom. These are called 'cumulus clouds'. They form when warm air bubbles upwards and reaches cold air higher in the atmosphere, and the water vapour in the air condenses.

Cumulonimbus clouds are heaped clouds that bring rain.

Cumulonimbus clouds

Cumulonimbus clouds, or thunderclouds, are very tall cumulus clouds. The bottom is low, and they can reach 15 kilometres in height. They form when cumulus clouds pile up and up, as more moist air rises. They become full of water drops low down and ice crystals high up. They usually bring rain and can also bring thunderstorms, lightning and even tornadoes.

Nimbostratus clouds

Nimbostratus clouds, or rain clouds, form a dull grey blanket of cloud in the sky. They are found at a fairly low level, and bring damp or wet weather. They are grey because the raindrops in them block the sunlight.

Cirrus clouds

Cirrus clouds, or ice clouds, are very high and are made of ice crystals. They make wispy, feathery patterns, which are created by winds blowing high in the atmosphere. Cirrus clouds do not bring rain. Cirrostratus clouds form flat ice **veils** across the sky.

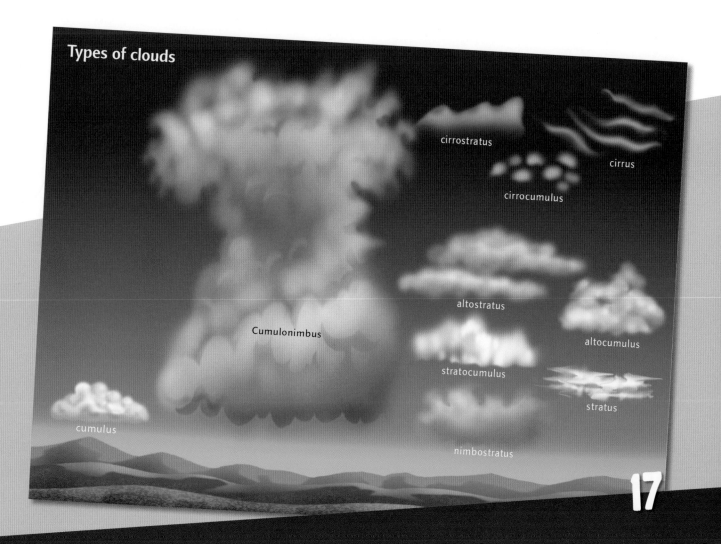

Types of clouds

cirrostratus

cirrus

cirrocumulus

altostratus

altocumulus

Cumulonimbus

stratocumulus

stratus

cumulus

nimbostratus

Precipitation

Water or ice that falls out of clouds is called 'precipitation'. Rain, drizzle, **hail**, snow and **ice pellets** are types of precipitation.

In clouds, when tiny drops of water bump into each other they can join together to make larger drops. These may become too heavy to remain in the atmosphere, and fall out of the clouds as rain. Rain that is made up of very tiny raindrops is known as 'drizzle'.

Hail and short showers

Raindrops in thunderclouds get blown upwards. It is much colder at these heights, and the raindrops freeze onto ice crystals, which can then form balls of ice called 'hailstones'. If these are heavy enough they fall to the ground, or they can be thrown to the ground by winds. If they melt on the way down, they fall as short rain **showers**.

Weather Report

Large hailstones can damage cars and buildings, and are dangerous to people.

Hailstones move up and down within the thunderclouds several times. Each time they fall and rise, more water is frozen onto their surface. Hailstones can become quite large.

Hailstorms can cause very dangerous driving conditions.

Steady rain, snow and ice pellets

Steady rain comes from low, grey nimbostratus clouds. These clouds are full of heavy water drops. If rain clouds are in a cold enough area, such as in the mountains, they will contain ice crystals that grow into snowflakes. The snowflakes may melt as they fall, giving steady rain, or they may fall to the ground in the form of snow.

If steady rain falls through icy-cold air that is close to the ground it can freeze, and make ice pellets.

A rainbow is caused by sunlight shining on water drops. The raindrops split the sunlight into the colours red, orange, yellow, green, blue, indigo and violet.

Weather Report

Falls of ice pellets are called 'sleet' in North America. In other places, such as Australia and England, sleet means a mixture of rain and snow.

Air movements

Air is made of very tiny particles. They are so small we cannot see them. They are far apart and they move around quickly.

Air pressure

Air pressure is the weight of the air when it pushes on the ground and other things such as people and objects. Air pressure is all around us. The air over a large area can have much the same air pressure and temperature. This air then moves all together in one large body.

Low pressure

When the air is warmed, the particles move faster and become further apart. This makes the air lighter and the air pressure drops. The warmed air rises upwards, because it weighs less. This often brings unsettled weather, such as wind and rain because the rising air cools and the water vapour condenses, which makes clouds. These bodies of air are known as 'depressions'.

Barometers are used to measure air pressure. This barometer is showing high pressure.

High pressure

When the air is cooled, the particles slow down and move closer together. This makes the air heavier and the air pressure increases. This cooled air sinks towards the ground. No clouds can form because the air warms up and dries out as it sinks. This usually brings clear skies and calm weather.

Air currents

As the Sun heats the land, the air above it is warmed. This warm air rises up and is replaced by cooler air drawn in from nearby. These movements of air are called 'air currents'.

When cooler air is trapped below warmer air, pollution can be trapped close to the ground. This gives us smog.

This glider is riding a warm rising air current.

Wind

Wind is the movement of the air. It is a stronger movement than a gentle air current. Wind is caused by air pressure changes and by the spinning of Earth.

Changes in air pressure

Large bodies of air can develop high or low pressure. When this happens, air flows from areas of high pressure to areas of low pressure. This is because the particles in the high-pressure air push harder than the particles in the low-pressure air. This air movement is called 'wind'.

Wind direction

The direction of the wind can make a big difference to the weather in an area. The wind may bring hot, dry weather if it blows off a hot **desert**, or it may bring wet weather if it blows off an ocean.

Kite flying is a fun way to enjoy windy conditions.

These palm trees show the strength of the wind.

Spiralling winds

Winds move in a spiralling pattern around areas with high and low air pressure. This is because Earth spins on its axis.

Wind spirals into large bodies of low-pressure air. North of the equator, wind spirals towards low-pressure air in a **counter-clockwise** direction. South of the equator, wind spirals towards low-pressure air in a **clockwise** direction. Winds do not spiral at the equator.

Wind spirals out of large bodies of high-pressure air. North of the equator, wind spirals away from high-pressure air in a clockwise direction. South of the equator, wind spirals away from high-pressure air in a counter-clockwise direction.

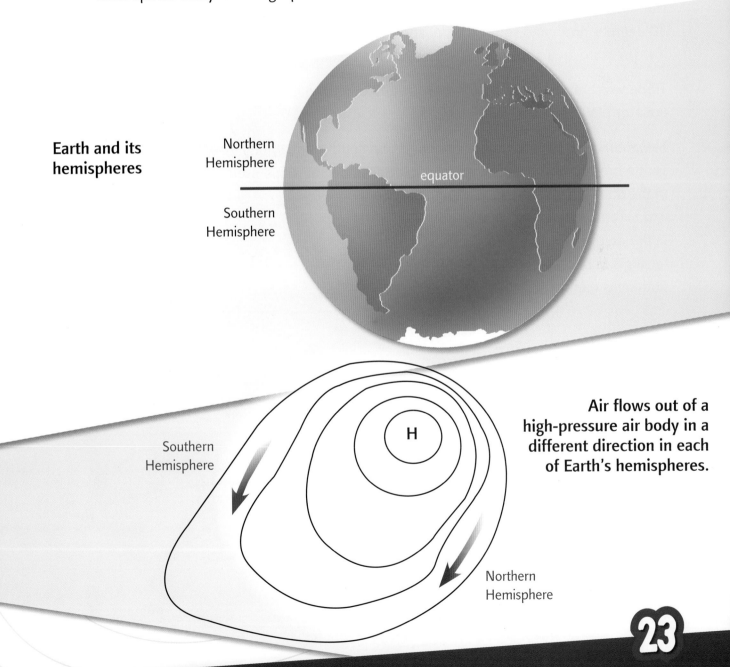

Earth and its hemispheres

Northern Hemisphere

equator

Southern Hemisphere

Southern Hemisphere

H

Northern Hemisphere

Air flows out of a high-pressure air body in a different direction in each of Earth's hemispheres.

Global winds

There is a pattern of wind movement in Earth's atmosphere. This causes winds that are the same year after year. These winds are known as 'global winds'.

Trade winds and doldrums

Warm air rises over the **tropics**. It reaches the top of the troposphere, where it can rise no further. It gradually cools and sinks to Earth's surface at the **latitudes** 30 degrees north and south. This pushes some air from these latitudes to the low-pressure area at the equator. This airflow is known as the 'trade winds'.

Trade winds above the equator blow from the north-east, and trade winds below the equator blow from the south-east.

The area at the equator where the north and south trade winds meet has only gentle breezes and is known as the 'doldrums'. Sailing ships used to get stuck in the doldrums for weeks, waiting for some wind. Today, the saying 'being in the doldrums' means feeling sad because nothing is happening.

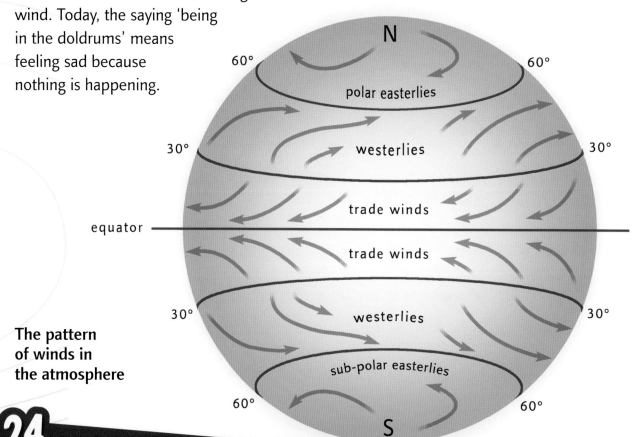

The pattern of winds in the atmosphere

N
60°   60°
polar easterlies
30°   30°
westerlies
trade winds
equator
trade winds
30°   30°
westerlies
sub-polar easterlies
60°   60°
S

Other winds

Winds that blow between the latitudes of 30 and 60 degrees north and south are called 'westerlies'. They blow from the south-west in the Northern Hemisphere and the north-west in the Southern Hemisphere. Many people live within these latitudes, so the westerlies bring the weather to many of Earth's people.

Polar easterlies occur between the poles and 60 degrees north and south. There are not many people affected by these winds.

Weather Report

Jet streams were first discovered during World War II. Pilots who regularly flew between the United Kingdom and the United States noticed that it was quicker to fly to the UK, reporting tailwinds of over 100 miles per hour. These winds blew in narrow ribbons and were named 'jet streams'.

Jet streams

Jet streams are rivers of fast winds that flow at the top of the troposphere. Jet streams are found between the boundaries of warm and cold air. Most of the jet streams blow from the west, but their locations change over time.

These clouds high in the atmosphere are blown into streaks by strong jet stream winds.

The oceans

Water in Earth's oceans and seas flow in rivers known as 'ocean currents'. There are warm currents and cold currents. These currents have a huge effect on the world's climates, which in turn affect the living conditions on land for humans, animals and plants.

The air that passes over warm currents is warmed up. As it warms it rises, and collects moisture from the sea. When this moist air is blown over land, it brings rain.

The air that passes over cold currents is cooled, and carries very little moisture. When this air is blown over land it is dry, and will not bring much, if any, rain. This wind gives these areas cool sea **breezes**.

Ocean currents around Earth

warm current →
cold current →

El Niño brought floods to this city in Brazil, South America.

El Niño

El Niño is the name of a weather pattern that takes place every few years around the Pacific Ocean. It is caused by changes in ocean currents.

Normally there is cold water on the east side of the Pacific, along the coasts of North and South America. There is warm water on the west side, around Asia and eastern Australia. This normally brings dry air to land around the eastern Pacific and rain to land around the western Pacific. This water–weather system is known as 'La Niña'.

During El Niño, the cold and warm water switch locations. The trade winds weaken or head east. This upsets the world's weather. El Niño brings drought to eastern Australia, New Zealand and parts of Asia, and rains and floods to western North and South America.

El Niño brought drought to this valley in Tasmania, Australia.

Storms

An approaching
thunderstorm

We say there is a storm when there is strong wind, together with rain, hail, thunder, lightning or snow. Storms are often caused by the collision of air bodies.

Warm and cold fronts

A weather front is the border between two bodies of air that have different air pressures, temperatures and humidities. Weather fronts often bring stormy weather. Cold fronts often come from the west, and warm fronts usually come from the equator.

When a cold front approaches, high-pressure air pushes into warm, low-pressure air. The warm air is lifted up very quickly and cumulonimbus clouds can form. This may lead to showers and thunderstorms.

When a warm front approaches, warm air slides over colder air close to the ground. Cumulus clouds appear, then stratus clouds bring rain, and it can become windy.

Cold front: cool air moves towards warm air, and slides below it.

Warm front: warm air moves towards cool air, and slides over it.

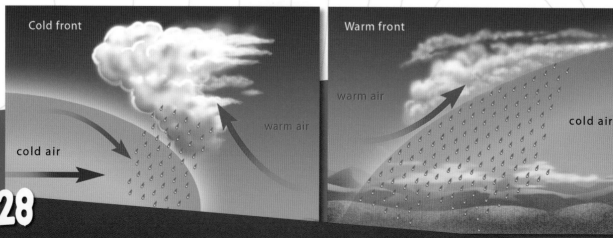

Cold front

cold air

warm air

Warm front

warm air

cold air

Tropical storms

Tropical storms form over warm tropical seas in hot weather. Some move over land. They are also known as 'hurricanes', 'cyclones' and 'typhoons'. They bring extreme wind, rain and floods, and are very dangerous.

In a tropical storm, warm air that contains lots of water vapour rises fast, creating a low-pressure area. More air, also full of water vapour, rushes in below to replace it, and spirals upwards. Cumulonimbus clouds form quickly as the rising moist air cools.

The centre of a tropical storm is still. The winds spiralling inwards and upwards make a rotating wall of cloud around it. This wind can be very fast.

Tornadoes

Tornadoes are rotating funnels of cloud that sometimes come from the base of thunderclouds. They are very dangerous because they can suck up almost anything in their path, and they move along quickly and unpredictably.

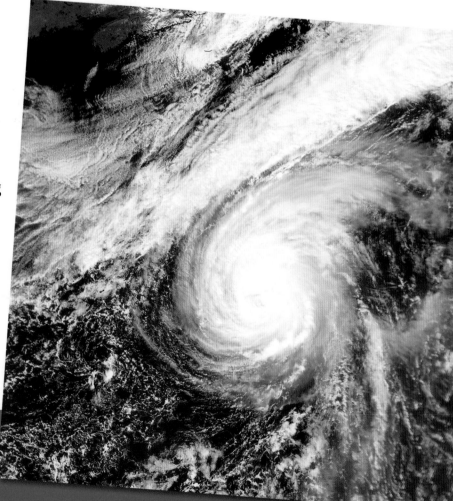

In 2005, the winds in Hurricane Dennis reached speeds of 240 kilometres per hour.

Weather wonders

The average temperature of the atmosphere at sea level is 15 degrees Celsius.

Water freezes at 0 degrees Celsius. Water boils at 100 degrees Celsius.

The foggiest place in the world is the Grand Banks off the island of Newfoundland, Canada.

Raindrops are round, unless they are very large, then they are flat across the bottom or doughnut shaped. The largest raindrops have been measured at about 5 millimetres across.

The troposphere reaches 15 kilometres above the ground over the equator and 8 kilometres above the ground over the North and South Poles.

On average, the United States has about 1200 tornadoes per year.

Storm surges from tropical storms can cause floods up to 40 kilometres inland.

Glossary

axis imaginary line through the middle of Earth, from top to bottom

breezes gentle winds

carbon dioxide gas produced by burning petrol, coal and natural gas

Celsius a temperature scale

clockwise movement in the same direction as clock hands

condenses changes from a gas to a liquid

counter-clockwise movement in the opposite direction to clock hands

crystals tiny particles of a pure substance

desert very dry area that receives very little rainfall

evaporates changes from a liquid to a gas

gases substances made of tiny invisible particles that are far apart

hail falls of ice balls from thunderclouds

hemisphere half a sphere; either the top (north) or bottom (south) half of Earth

ice pellets ice balls that are frozen raindrops

latitudes imaginary lines around Earth, that give the location of a place on Earth north or south of the equator

meteors large rocks that fly through space

North Pole northernmost point on Earth

orbiting a planet following a curved path

ozone kind of oxygen gas found in the stratosphere

radiation invisible energy rays, such as heat

rays beams of energy, such as heat

showers rain that does not last long

solar system the Sun and the planets that move around it

South Pole southernmost point on Earth

storm surges higher sea level caused by a storm

tropics area on and near Earth's equator

ultraviolet light type of invisible light

veils very thin sheets of something

water vapour water in the form of a gas

Index